Your Commitment, Dedication and Passion for Your Work are Really Appreciated.

Thank You for Giving 100% Every Day!

*"keep taking chances - make life a
beautiful experience and never give up"*

Date: /   /

_____

_____

_____

_____

_____

_____

_____

_____

_____

_____

_____

_____

_____

_____

_____

_____

_____

_____

_____

TODAY I FEEL GRATEFUL FOR:

"Life is like a piano. Anyone can play a song through meaningless repetition, but it takes passion to play a masterpiece" — *Anonymous*

Date: /   /

TODAY I FEEL GRATEFUL FOR:

"You have to put up with the rain to get the rainbow" — Anonymous

Date: /   /

_____

_____

_____

_____

_____

_____

_____

_____

_____

_____

_____

_____

_____

_____

_____

_____

_____

_____

TODAY I FEEL GRATEFUL FOR:

"It is one life whether we spend it laughing or weeping" — Anonymous

Date: /   /

TODAY I FEEL GRATEFUL FOR:

"The giant oak is an acorn that held its ground"
— Anonymous

Date: /   /
_____

_____
_____
_____
_____
_____
_____
_____
_____
_____
_____
_____
_____
_____
_____
_____
_____
_____
_____
_____

TODAY I FEEL GRATEFUL FOR:

"Try and fail, but don't fail to try"
— Anonymous

Date: /   /

TODAY I FEEL GRATEFUL FOR:

"There is nothing so powerful as the truth"
— Anonymous

Date: /   /

_____

_____

_____

_____

_____

_____

_____

_____

_____

_____

_____

_____

_____

_____

_____

_____

_____

_____

TODAY I FEEL GRATEFUL FOR:

"Have dreams and dream big! Dream without fear"

Date: /   /

_____

_____

_____

_____

_____

_____

_____

_____

_____

_____

_____

_____

_____

_____

_____

_____

_____

_____

_____

_____

TODAY I FEEL GRATEFUL FOR:

"Hard things are put in our way, not to stop us, but to call out our courage and strength" — *Anonymous*

Date: / /

_____
_____
_____
_____
_____
_____
_____
_____
_____
_____
_____
_____
_____
_____
_____
_____
_____
_____
_____

TODAY I FEEL GRATEFUL FOR:

"Never forget what is worth remembering or remember what is best forgotten" — *Anonymous*

Date: /   /

TODAY I FEEL GRATEFUL FOR:

*"Turn your dreams into reality with
the power of your imagination"*

Date: /   /

TODAY I FEEL GRATEFUL FOR:

"Believe in miracles but above all believe in yourself!"

Date: /   /

TODAY I FEEL GRATEFUL FOR:

"A strong person knows that the joy of life is not found in the destination but in the journey"

Date: /   /

TODAY I FEEL GRATEFUL FOR:

"A diamond is a chunk of coal that made good under pressure" — *Anonymous*

Date: /   /

TODAY I FEEL GRATEFUL FOR:

"Let your dreams be as big as your desire to succeed"

Date: /   /

_____

_____

_____

_____

_____

_____

_____

_____

_____

_____

_____

_____

_____

_____

_____

_____

_____

_____

_____

_____

TODAY I FEEL GRATEFUL FOR:

"A strong person is the one who makes significant decisions in emotional circumstances"

Date: /   /

TODAY I FEEL GRATEFUL FOR:

"They say I dream too big. I say they think too small" - Unknown

Date: /   /

_____

_____

_____

_____

_____

_____

_____

_____

_____

_____

_____

_____

_____

_____

_____

_____

_____

_____

TODAY I FEEL GRATEFUL FOR:

"Adversity is the springboard to great achievement"
- Anonymous

Date: /   /

_____

_____

_____

_____

_____

_____

_____

_____

_____

_____

_____

_____

_____

_____

_____

_____

TODAY I FEEL GRATEFUL FOR:

"An obstacle is something you see when you take your eyes off the goal" - Anonymous

Date: /   /
_____

_____

_____

_____

_____

_____

_____

_____

_____

_____

_____

_____

_____

_____

_____

_____

_____

_____

_____

TODAY I FEEL GRATEFUL FOR:

"Don't ever let your problems become an excuse"
- Anonymous

Date: /   /

TODAY I FEEL GRATEFUL FOR:

"Every great achievement was once impossible"
- Anonymous

Date: /   /

TODAY I FEEL GRATEFUL FOR:

"Always believe in yourself and your inner power"

Date: /   /

_____

_____

_____

_____

_____

_____

_____

_____

_____

_____

_____

_____

_____

_____

_____

_____

TODAY I FEEL GRATEFUL FOR:

"Never let defeat have the last word" — Anonymous

Date: /   /

_____

_____

_____

_____

_____

_____

_____

_____

_____

_____

_____

_____

_____

_____

_____

_____

_____

_____

_____

TODAY I FEEL GRATEFUL FOR:

"All our tomorrows depend on today" — *Anonymous*

Date: /   /

TODAY I FEEL GRATEFUL FOR:

"Don't just wait for life to happen, make it happen!"

Date: /   /

_____

_____

_____

_____

_____

_____

_____

_____

_____

_____

_____

_____

_____

_____

_____

_____

_____

_____

TODAY I FEEL GRATEFUL FOR:

"Your only limitation is your imagination"
— Anonymous

Date: /   /

TODAY I FEEL GRATEFUL FOR:

"Your driving force and your power lies within you and the size of your dreams, never give up!"

Date: /   /

TODAY I FEEL GRATEFUL FOR:

*"Happiness is not something you get,
but something you do" — Anonymous*

Date: /   /

TODAY I FEEL GRATEFUL FOR:

"Have the courage to live. Anyone can die"
— Anonymous

Date: /   /

TODAY I FEEL GRATEFUL FOR:

"Wherever you go, go with all your heart"
- Confucius

Date: / /

TODAY I FEEL GRATEFUL FOR:

"The winner always has a plan;
The loser always has an excuse" — Anonymous

Date: /   /

_____

_____
_____
_____
_____
_____
_____
_____
_____
_____
_____
_____
_____
_____
_____
_____
_____

TODAY I FEEL GRATEFUL FOR:

"Your dreams and your goals are the seeds of your own success"

Date: /   /

TODAY I FEEL GRATEFUL FOR:

"We are limited, not by our abilities, but by our vision"
— Anonymous

Date: / /

_____

_____
_____
_____
_____
_____
_____
_____
_____
_____
_____
_____
_____
_____
_____
_____
_____
_____
_____

TODAY I FEEL GRATEFUL FOR:

"Never give up, keep going no matter what!"

Date: /   /

TODAY I FEEL GRATEFUL FOR:

*"Don't go into something to test the waters,
go into things to make waves"* — *Anonymous*

Date: /   /

TODAY I FEEL GRATEFUL FOR:

"If you never give up you become unbeatable, just keep going!"

Date: /   /

TODAY I FEEL GRATEFUL FOR:

"Anything worth doing is worth doing well"
— Anonymous

Date: /   /

_____

_____

_____

_____

_____

_____

_____

_____

_____

_____

_____

_____

_____

_____

_____

_____

_____

TODAY I FEEL GRATEFUL FOR:

"There are no limits to what you can achieve
if you believe in your dreams"

Date: /   /

TODAY I FEEL GRATEFUL FOR:

"Live, love, laugh" — Anonymous

Date: /   /

_____

TODAY I FEEL GRATEFUL FOR:

"Don't let yesterday's disappointments, overshadow tomorrow's achievements" — *Anonymous*

Date: /   /

TODAY I FEEL GRATEFUL FOR:

"When you feel you are defeated, just remember, you have the power to move on, it is all in your mind"

Date: /   /

TODAY I FEEL GRATEFUL FOR:

*"Don't be pushed by your problems.
Be led by your dreams"* — Anonymous

Date: /   /

TODAY I FEEL GRATEFUL FOR:

"Some pursue happiness – others create it"
— Anonymous

Date: /   /

_____

_____

_____

_____

_____

_____

_____

_____

_____

_____

_____

_____

_____

_____

_____

_____

_____

TODAY I FEEL GRATEFUL FOR:

"Don't just dream your dreams, make them happen!"

Date: /   /

TODAY I FEEL GRATEFUL FOR:

"Laughter is the shock absorber that softens and minimizes the bumps of life" — *Anonymous*

Date: /   /

TODAY I FEEL GRATEFUL FOR:

"Opportunity comes to those who never give up"

Date: /   /

TODAY I FEEL GRATEFUL FOR:

"Dream is not what you see in sleep, dream is the thing which does not let you sleep" — Anonymous

Date: /   /

_____

_____

_____

_____

_____

_____

_____

_____

_____

_____

_____

_____

_____

_____

_____

_____

TODAY I FEEL GRATEFUL FOR:

"You are the creator of your own opportunities"

Date: /   /

_____

_____

_____

_____

_____

_____

_____

_____

_____

_____

_____

_____

_____

_____

_____

_____

_____

_____

_____

_____

TODAY I FEEL GRATEFUL FOR:

"If you want to feel rich, just count all the things you have that money can't buy" - Anonymous

Date: /   /

TODAY I FEEL GRATEFUL FOR:

*"Every achievement starts with a dream
and a goal in mind"*

Date: /   /

TODAY I FEEL GRATEFUL FOR:

"Dreams don't come true. Dreams are true"
— Anonymous

Date: /   /

_____

_____

_____

_____

_____

_____

_____

_____

_____

_____

_____

_____

_____

_____

_____

_____

TODAY I FEEL GRATEFUL FOR:

"Dreams are the energy that power your life"

Date: /   /

_____

_____

_____

_____

_____

_____

_____

_____

_____

_____

_____

_____

_____

_____

_____

_____

_____

_____

_____

TODAY I FEEL GRATEFUL FOR:

*"Remember yesterday, dream of tomorrow,
but live for today"* — *Anonymous*

Date: /   /

TODAY I FEEL GRATEFUL FOR:

"Never stop dreaming" - Anonymous

Date: /   /

_____

_____

_____

_____

_____

_____

_____

_____

_____

_____

_____

_____

_____

_____

_____

_____

_____

TODAY I FEEL GRATEFUL FOR:

*"To live a creative life, we must lose our fear
of being wrong" - Anonymous*

Date: /   /

TODAY I FEEL GRATEFUL FOR:

"Dreams are the foundation to our imagination and success"

Date: /   /

TODAY I FEEL GRATEFUL FOR:

"If you do what you always did,
you will get what you always got" - Anonymous

Date: / /

TODAY I FEEL GRATEFUL FOR:

"Be brave, fight for what you believe in and make your dreams a reality." - Anonymous

Date: /   /

TODAY I FEEL GRATEFUL FOR:

"Don't raise your voice, improve your argument"
- Anonymous

Date: /   /

TODAY I FEEL GRATEFUL FOR:

*"It's not what you look at that matters,
it's what you see" - Anonymous*

Date: /   /

TODAY I FEEL GRATEFUL FOR:

"Let your dreams be bigger than your fears and your actions louder than your words" - Anonymous

Date: /   /

TODAY I FEEL GRATEFUL FOR:

"There is always something to be thankful for"

Date: / /

TODAY I FEEL GRATEFUL FOR:

"Dream. Believe. Create. Succeed" - Anonymous

Date: /   /

_____

_____

_____

_____

_____

_____

_____

_____

_____

_____

_____

_____

_____

_____

_____

_____

TODAY I FEEL GRATEFUL FOR:

"Your mind is a powerful thing. When you fill it with positive thoughts, your life will start to change"

Date: /   /

TODAY I FEEL GRATEFUL FOR:

"If you have big dreams you will always have big reasons to wake up every day"

Date: /   /

_____

_____
_____
_____
_____
_____
_____
_____
_____
_____
_____
_____
_____
_____
_____
_____
_____
_____
_____

TODAY I FEEL GRATEFUL FOR:

"Nobody can make you happy until you're happy with yourself"

Date: /   /

_____

_____

_____

_____

_____

_____

_____

_____

_____

_____

_____

_____

_____

_____

_____

_____

_____

TODAY I FEEL GRATEFUL FOR:

"To achieve our dreams we must first overcome our fear of failure"

Date: /   /

TODAY I FEEL GRATEFUL FOR:

"You have three choices: give up, give in, give it all you've got"

Date: /   /

_____

_____

_____

_____

_____

_____

_____

_____

_____

_____

_____

_____

_____

_____

_____

_____

TODAY I FEEL GRATEFUL FOR:

*"When life knocks you down, roll over
and look at the stars"*

Date: /   /
_____

_____

_____

_____

_____

_____

_____

_____

_____

_____

_____

_____

_____

_____

_____

_____

_____

_____

_____

TODAY I FEEL GRATEFUL FOR:

"Have faith in the future but above all in yourself"

Date: /   /

_____
_____
_____
_____
_____
_____
_____
_____
_____
_____
_____
_____
_____
_____
_____
_____
_____
_____
_____
_____
_____

TODAY I FEEL GRATEFUL FOR:

"Kindness makes you the most beautiful person in the world, no matter what you look like"

Date: /   /
_____

_____
_____
_____
_____
_____
_____
_____
_____
_____
_____
_____
_____
_____
_____
_____
_____
_____
_____

TODAY I FEEL GRATEFUL FOR:

"Just when the caterpillar thought her life was over, she began to fly"

Date: / /

_____

TODAY I FEEL GRATEFUL FOR:

*"Your future is created by what you do today
not tomorrow"* - Anonymous

Date: /   /

TODAY I FEEL GRATEFUL FOR:

"Every time you subtract negative from your life, you make room for more positive"

Date: /   /

_____
_____
_____
_____
_____
_____
_____
_____
_____
_____
_____
_____
_____
_____
_____
_____
_____
_____

TODAY I FEEL GRATEFUL FOR:

"Make your own destiny. Don't wait for it to come to you, life is not a rehearsal" — *Anonymous*

Date: /   /

TODAY I FEEL GRATEFUL FOR:

"Sometimes life will test you but remember this: when you walk up a mountain, your legs get stronger"

Date: /   /

TODAY I FEEL GRATEFUL FOR:

"It's better to have an impossible dream than no dream at all" – Anonymous

Date: /   /

TODAY I FEEL GRATEFUL FOR:

"Success is not final; failure is not fatal.
It is the courage to continue that counts"

Date: /   /

TODAY I FEEL GRATEFUL FOR:

*"Happiness is not something you get,
but something you do"* — Anonymous

Date: /   /

TODAY I FEEL GRATEFUL FOR:

*"The less you respond to negativity,
the more peaceful your life becomes"*

Date: /   /

TODAY I FEEL GRATEFUL FOR:

"Don't wait for the perfect moment.
Take the moment and make it perfect"

Date: /   /

_____

_____
_____
_____
_____
_____
_____
_____
_____
_____
_____
_____
_____
_____
_____
_____
_____
_____

TODAY I FEEL GRATEFUL FOR:

*"Do something today that your future self
will thank you for"*

Date: /   /

_____

_____

_____

_____

_____

_____

_____

_____

_____

_____

_____

_____

_____

_____

_____

_____

TODAY I FEEL GRATEFUL FOR:

*"Don't let the world change your smile,
let your smile change the world"*

Date: /   /

TODAY I FEEL GRATEFUL FOR:

"The best things in life aren't things"

Date: /   /

TODAY I FEEL GRATEFUL FOR:

*"Instead of giving myself reasons why I can't,
I give myself reasons why I can"*

Date: /   /

TODAY I FEEL GRATEFUL FOR:

"A strong woman stands up for herself,
a stronger woman stands up for others"

Date: /   /

TODAY I FEEL GRATEFUL FOR:

"Everyday is another chance to change your life"
- Anonymous

Date: /   /
_____

_____

_____

_____

_____

_____

_____

_____

_____

_____

_____

_____

_____

_____

_____

_____

TODAY I FEEL GRATEFUL FOR:

*"Every single morning we get a chance
to begin again"* - Anonymous

Date: /   /

_____

_____

_____

_____

_____

_____

_____

_____

_____

_____

_____

_____

_____

_____

_____

_____

_____

_____

TODAY I FEEL GRATEFUL FOR:

*"Don't let a bad day make you feel like
you have a bad life."* – Unknown

Date: / /

TODAY I FEEL GRATEFUL FOR:

"Failure doesn't come from falling down. Failure comes from not getting up" – Unknown

Date: /   /

TODAY I FEEL GRATEFUL FOR:

"The only person you should try to be better than is the person you were yesterday" – Unknown

Date: /   /

_____

_____

_____

_____

_____

_____

_____

_____

_____

_____

_____

_____

_____

_____

_____

_____

_____

_____

_____

TODAY I FEEL GRATEFUL FOR:

"Even the darkest nights will end and the sun will rise"
– Unknown

Date: /   /

TODAY I FEEL GRATEFUL FOR:

"Even the darkest nights will end and the sun will rise"
– Unknown

Date: /   /

TODAY I FEEL GRATEFUL FOR:

"Our greatest glory lies not in never failing but in rising every time we fail" – *Confucius*

Date: /   /

_____

_____

_____

_____

_____

_____

_____

_____

_____

_____

_____

_____

_____

_____

_____

_____

_____

_____

TODAY I FEEL GRATEFUL FOR:

"Forget all the reasons it won't work and believe the one reason that it will" – Unknown

Date: /   /

_____

_____

_____

_____

_____

_____

_____

_____

_____

_____

_____

_____

_____

_____

_____

_____

_____

TODAY I FEEL GRATEFUL FOR:

"The biggest failure you can have in life is making the mistake of never trying at all" – Unknown

Date: /   /

TODAY I FEEL GRATEFUL FOR:

*"A journey of a thousand miles must begin
with a single step"* – Lao Tzu

Date: /   /

TODAY I FEEL GRATEFUL FOR:

"No dreamer is ever too small;
no dream is ever too big" – Anonymous

Date: /   /

_____
_____
_____
_____
_____
_____
_____
_____
_____
_____
_____
_____
_____
_____
_____
_____
_____
_____
_____
_____

TODAY I FEEL GRATEFUL FOR:

"Don't be pushed by your problems.
Be led by your dreams" — Anonymous

Date: /   /

TODAY I FEEL GRATEFUL FOR:

"Try and fail, but don't fail to try" — Anonymous

Date: /   /

_____

_____

_____

_____

_____

_____

_____

_____

_____

_____

_____

_____

_____

_____

_____

_____

_____

TODAY I FEEL GRATEFUL FOR:

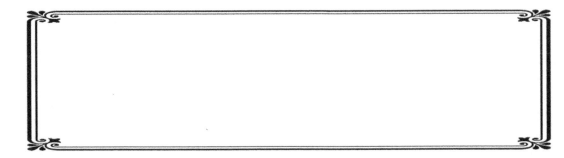

"Follow your heart and your dreams will come true"
– Anonymous

Date: /   /

TODAY I FEEL GRATEFUL FOR:

"Believe in yourself and you will be unstoppable"

Date: /   /

TODAY I FEEL GRATEFUL FOR:

"Make each day count, you will never have this day again"

Date: /   /

TODAY I FEEL GRATEFUL FOR:

"To be the best you must be able to handle the worst"
- Anonymous

Date: /   /

TODAY I FEEL GRATEFUL FOR:

"Wherever you go, go with all your heart" - Confucius

Date: /   /

TODAY I FEEL GRATEFUL FOR:

"Don't Let Anyone Dull Your Sparkle"

Date: /   /

TODAY I FEEL GRATEFUL FOR:

"Nothing worth having comes easy" - Anonymous

Date: /   /

_____

_____

_____

_____

_____

_____

_____

_____

_____

_____

_____

_____

_____

_____

_____

_____

_____

_____

TODAY I FEEL GRATEFUL FOR:

THANK YOU FOR USING THIS
JOURNAL – NOTEBOOK
PLEASE LET US KNOW
IF YOU LIKED IT
BY WRTING A REVIEW.

THANK YOU!

Diana Creations

Made in the USA
Coppell, TX
09 January 2021

47821604R20063